DOROTHY HOLE

THE COAST GUARD AND YOU

CRESTWOOD HOUSE
NEW YORK
MAXWELL MACMILLAN CANADA
TORONTO
MAXWELL MACMILLAN INTERNATIONAL
NEW YORK • OXFORD • SINGAPORE • SYDNEY

ACKNOWLEDGMENTS

Many thanks to Dennis Mark, Petty Officer, First Class, United States Coast Guard and Paul A. Milligan, Lieutenant Commander, United States Coast Guard

DEDICATION

For my daughter, Elizabeth Hole Vidal

PHOTO CREDITS: *Photos courtesy of U.S. Coast Guard.*

Cover design, text design and production: William E. Frost Associates Ltd.

Library of Congress Cataloging-in-Publication Data

Hole, Dorothy.
  The Coast Guard and you / by Dorothy Hole. —1st ed.
    p. cm. — (The armed forces)
  Summary: Discusses life in the United States Coast Guard, how to join this branch of the armed forces, and how to decide if serving is the right career choice for you.
    ISBN 0-89686-766-8
    1. United States. Coast Guard — Vocational guidance — Juvenile literature. [1. United States. Coast Guard — Vocational guidance. 2. Vocational guidance.] I. Title. II. Series: Hole, Dorothy. Armed forces.
VG53.H65 1993
359.9'7'02373 — dc20   92-9775

CRESTWOOD HOUSE
MACMILLAN PUBLISHING COMPANY
866 Third Avenue
New York, NY 10022

MAXWELL MACMILLAN CANADA, INC.
1200 Eglinton Avenue East
Suite 200
Don Mills, Ontario M3C 3N1

Macmillan Publishing Company is part of the Maxwell Communication Group of Companies
First Edition
Printed in the United States of America

10 9 8 7 6 5 4 3 2 1

CONTENTS

Members of Coast Guard search and rescue teams are trained to operate on a moment's notice to protect and rescue lives in U.S. waters.

CHAPTER ONE

IS THE COAST GUARD FOR YOU?

A sudden loud blaring horn jolts you awake. It is 2:00 A.M. Your heart races. You don't stop to wonder what's happened. You grab your boots and run toward the dock.

It is cold and dark. In under five minutes—more like three or four—your motor lifeboat pushes off from the dock. While under way, you and three other Coast Guardsmen put on your orange survival suits. You are a member of a crew on a search and rescue mission. You are responding to one of the 80,000 calls the Coast Guard receives each year for help on the water.

This time two fishing boats have collided on the Pacific Ocean, many miles offshore from Humboldt Bay in northern California. One boat is sinking fast.

While you speed toward the scene, your skipper and his crew must keep in touch by radio communication to learn more facts. How fast is the boat sinking? How many people on board? Any other vessels nearby to help? Any serious injuries?

The Coast Guard is the lead agency to respond to the threat of coastal pollution. Here, a Coast Guard environmental protection worker examines the shoreline after an oil spill in Huntington Beach, California.

Twenty minutes later your lifeboat arrives at the scene, just in time to see the smaller of the fishing boats sink under the waves. Most of the fishermen and women are safe on the larger fishing boat. One man is still thrashing in the water, unseen by anyone on the boat.

You and your crew pick him out of the water. When you return to your bed at the Coast Guard Station, you know you've made a difference. How many people can go to sleep knowing they've saved a life?

———

You've always longed for action and adventure. If you sign up to join the Coast Guard, you make an important decision. You want that action to have a purpose—not action for the sake of action. No bungee jumping just for the thrill. You believe it's much more satisfying to jump from a helicopter to pluck a drowning man from the ocean or to rescue a family from a burning motorboat.

Each year the Coast Guard saves the lives of approximately 5,000 people. More than 140,000 are helped in some way when they find themselves in a dangerous situation. If you're assigned to the Coast Guard **Search and Rescue Operations**, you have a busy life!

Both men and women are accepted by the Coast Guard. In fact, every job in the Coast Guard is open to both men and women. Sometimes appropriate facilities for women are not available, but if they are, both sexes may serve in every capacity.

Should you join? Only you can decide. Rescue work can be dangerous. So can cleaning up the ocean after an oil spill. And being part of a team stopping illegal drug smugglers can be especially risky.

Do you know how you would react to danger? Have you ever lived away from home? Perhaps settling down in a new place will not be as much fun as you thought. The Coast Guard considers you an adult and treats you like one. No one is around to see that your clothes are clean, your bills paid and that you report for duty on time.

In other words, the Coast Guard expects and demands that you accept responsibility. This service places a great deal of responsibility on enlisted personnel; in some respects, more than the other services.

Are you cut out for a life that is very demanding? Exciting as search and rescue sounds, you may spend hours out on the ocean trying to find a lost person. You may have to help a crippled vessel. You may spend the night hunting for a missing boat or fighting a fire on a ship. It's exceedingly hard work. Are you up to it?

You will be reassigned every few years. This means you have to move, no matter how much you like where you're living. You may be assigned to a cold area—and you hate freezing weather! Or where it's hot, and you can't stand being in the sun.

How are you at taking orders? In the Coast Guard there can be no questioning an order. Someone's life may depend on how fast you act. There are people who rebel at being told what to do. Are you one of them? If so, the Coast Guard is not for you.

One more thing to consider. You will be spending a great deal of time on a boat. There is a good chance that you will be assigned to a small one, under 65 feet. You and three others make up the crew. It's rugged work. You might spend your whole 24-hour shift bobbing around on the ocean. Have you ever done any boating in rough weather? There you are, rain, shine, sleet and hail. Think it over.

There are advantages and disadvantages—just as there are for every job. You have steady work with chance of promotion.

The concept of women in the Coast Guard is nothing new. The assignment of women to certain ratings and to duties afloat, however, is relatively recent.

The Coast Guard is made up of men and women who have dedicated a good portion of their lives to their country. Are you willing to commit yourself to the service of others? Think it over carefully before deciding.

You receive free medical and dental care. Each year you have a 30-day paid vacation.

If you do not live on a **base**, you receive extra money for housing and **subsistence** (food, heating). You have shopping privileges at all armed services **commissaries** (supermarkets) and **post exchanges** (department stores). That means you can buy whatever you wish on any army, navy, air force or marine base at lower prices at these government stores. You also have the right to use recreational facilities on all military bases. This includes swimming pools, tennis courts, gyms, movie theaters and libraries.

The Coast Guard offers to help with your tuition (cost) for any off-duty studies you undertake. In some instances, 100 percent of the tuition is paid for you. Under another program, the **Montgomery G.I. Bill**, you contribute $100 a month for the first year toward your education. The government adds $350 a month until the total reaches $12,600. The courses you study must be approved by the Coast Guard and the **Veterans Administration**.

One of the biggest benefits of joining is the learning of a skill. When you enter the civilian job market, an employer will know you've had excellent training. You've also had hands-on experience. This gives you an edge over other job applicants.

It all sounds great. Remember, though, you may find you don't like military life. Once you've signed on, you have to stick with it until your enlistment is up.

You want to learn more about joining the Coast Guard. How do you begin?

CHAPTER TWO

LEARNING ABOUT YOU ·

It's a good idea to talk it over with your school counselor. Your counselor knows you a lot better than you realize. Your teachers' records, showing your grades, attendance and special abilities, are open for your counselor to use. You may be advised, "Stay away from the armed services." Perhaps you'll be told, "The Coast Guard is perfect for you."

You should also discuss with your parents or guardians whether to join. Keep in mind that no matter what you are told, you are the one who will be making the decision. It's your life. If you decide to join, you must be *sure* in your own mind. Don't be talked into enlisting if you're not convinced. Your life could be miserable.

(Photo left)   How do you feel about taking orders? This recruit is being lectured about the importance of attention to detail after he failed to salute a company commander.

If you decide to go ahead, the first step is taking the **Armed Services Vocational Aptitude Battery (ASVAB)**. This test is necessary to sign up for any of the armed services. It lets the service of your choice—the Coast Guard—know your natural skills and interests and how far along you are in your studies. It's good to take, whether or not you join. You learn what

Members of the Coast Guard must stay in top physical shape and remain ready to defend the nation in emergency situations.

talents you have and this can help you choose a job in civilian life that you are able to do successfully.

The test is given at high schools. If yours doesn't offer the ASVAB, get in touch with a Coast Guard recruiter. Arrangements will be made for you to take it at another testing place.

"A test?" you think. "What if I fail?" The Coast Guard realizes you may not be a genius. You're not expected to know everything.

A wide variety of subjects are covered. Some of these are arithmetic, general science and auto and shop information. An example of numerical operations questions:

"60 ÷ 15 =

A. 3
B. 4
C. 5
D. 6"

Can you figure out the answer?

There is a minimum (lowest) grade below which you will not be accepted. Unlike school, where your grade cannot be changed, you can get a new grade by retaking the ASVAB, but you have to wait one month to retake it. If you need to, you can try again after six months.

Go to the library. Get out books on the ASVAB. Do the sample tests. Study them. See where you went wrong. These will help you when you take the real thing.

The Coast Guard wants you to know how you've done. A recruiter will go over the results of your ASVAB with you. You will learn your strong subjects and your weak ones. This will help you know what sort of job you might like to do in the Coast Guard.

Now you're ready to talk it over with a recruiter. First you will be told that the Coast Guard is different in many ways from the four other armed services (army, navy, air force and marines).

The Coast Guard is responsive to the public's needs through a variety of maritime operations. Here, an iceberg is being tracked in an effort to promote marine transportation.

The first job of the other services is defending the United States from enemy attack and fighting overseas when the United States becomes involved in a conflict. Time in those services is spent preparing for that type of emergency. They are under the command of the Department of Defense.

You are surprised to learn that that is not true of the Coast Guard. Although it is classified as the fifth armed service, it is under the Department of Transportation. The Coast Guard carries out four primary missions: **maritime** law enforcement, marine safety, environmental protection and military defense readiness. Within these missions are 12 operating programs that include those the Coast Guard is most recognized for, such as search and rescue, drug interdiction, hazardous chemical cleanup response and aids to navigation.

The Coast Guard does in peacetime exactly what it does in wartime, with the exception of fighting. During a war it can become—but not always is—a part of the navy. This is only done on orders of the president of the United States.

That's a lot of work for less than 40,000 people, the smallest number of any of the armed services.

Now you have an overview of the Coast Guard. If you enlist, what does all this mean to you?

When you take the Coast Guard oath, you are pledging yourself to your country and to the American people.

CHAPTER THREE

SIGNING UP

When you turned 18, you probably registered at the post office. To join the Coast Guard, you must be between the ages of 17 and 28. Proof of citizenship—your birth certificate—is needed. If you were born out of the country and your parents are Americans, you must have a legal document showing you're a United States citizen. If you were born out of the United States and your parents are *not* citizens, you must show proof that you entered the country legally for permanent residency and have a green card.

You can be married, divorced or single. However, if you have the sole custody of a child, you will not be eligible to join.

If you and a friend sign up together, the Coast Guard promises that you will go to **boot camp (recruit basic training)** together.

If you're a high school senior at least 17 years of age, with your parents' consent, you can enlist now but not report for duty until you have graduated. This **Delayed Entry Program** gives you up to one year to earn your high school diploma.

How long will you be in the Coast Guard? Four years is the least number of years you can serve. However, your contract will read eight years. It works like this: The first four years you are on **active service**. Of course, you can stay active longer if you want to. However, if you wish to return to **civilian** life after four years, you spend the remaining four years in the **inactive reserve** corps. This means you can be called up anytime during a war that the Coast Guard needs you but you have no other duties.

You want to know more about everyday life in the Coast Guard. What job will you be doing?

Your recruiter will discuss with you various jobs and how you fit into the Coast Guard's needs. Before you are assigned your job specialty, you first must go to basic training, known as boot camp.

Then you will serve with a unit, which is when your specialty is decided on. The Coast Guard unit to which you're assigned can be as small as one consisting of ten people or it can be at a large base.

While serving with a unit, you are urged to apply for a **Class "A" school**, where you will learn a specialty. You will not be sent to a Class "A" school until you have served with a unit, unless you have been guaranteed one when you enlisted. Specialties range from aviation electrician's mate and gunner's mate to sonar technician. Maybe you will specialize as a **yeoman**.

Either sex can be a yeoman. That person's duties are clerical and secretarial. Do you know how to type, operate a copy machine and file accurately? If so, you might consider becoming a yeoman. That skill might, in civilian life, lead to your being an office manager or administrative assistant.

The professional requirements of the Coast Guard increase as advances in technology are made. Education is provided on the latest ideas and equipment so that members can meet the Coast Guard's demand for excellence.

In fact, every job in the Coast Guard has a similar skill in civilian life. "Radarman?" you question. The answer: radar operator, air traffic controller and radio broadcasting are three career possibilities.

Once you are sure the Coast Guard is for you, you will be asked to sign an application. This is similar to a form you will sign wherever you apply for a job. This application has background questions about you and your family. If you don't know all the answers, take it home. Try to fill in all the blanks. This is *not* an enlistment contract. It merely lets the government know you are considering the Coast Guard as a career.

Of course, you must pass a physical exam. That is not done at the recruiting station. Once you are sure you want to join the Coast Guard, you go to the **Military Entrance Processing Station (MEPS)**.

CHAPTER FOUR

THE MEPS

You will discover whether or not you qualify to become a member of the Coast Guard at a MEPS. Here, if you have not already done so, you take the ASVAB. You have a physical exam. A security check is done on you, and you take the oath of enlistment. It is a big day and you should get a good sleep the night prior to reporting.

These stations are located in various large cities around the country. If you are unable to get to the one nearest your home, the Coast Guard arranges for your transportation there and back.

Don't forget to bring with you all the legal papers the recruiter has listed: social security card, birth certificate and whatever else is required.

If you live very far away, the Coast Guard pays for you to travel to and stay at a hotel the night before. At the hotel a bed check is made at 11:00 P.M.—your first taste of military life! You must be in your room by then. You are awakened at 3:30 A.M.

Between then and 4:00 A.M., when you eat breakfast, you must shower and put on clean clothes. After breakfast you must be in the hotel lobby by 5:00 A.M., when your transportation to the military processing station arrives.

By 6:30 A.M. you are waiting to have your physical. Provide the examining doctor with all the information he or she requests. If possible, have a copy of your medical record from your own doctor's files.

Do you wear glasses? The doctor will want to see a copy of the prescription. Your eyes are examined to discover if you are color-blind. This will not keep you out of the Coast Guard but it means there are certain jobs not open to you.

Have you had any serious illnesses? Broken bones? Undergone any major operations? Are you taking any prescribed medication? What about your teeth? Do you wear braces? The doctor will need to know all of this information.

Do not lie about alcohol or drug abuse. You will be tested for both. The Coast Guard doesn't want you if you use drugs. Prior felony arrests will also disqualify you. You will be tested for HIV, the virus which causes AIDS.

Once your physical is over, you move on to the **Entrance National Agency Checks (ENTNAC)**. As the Coast Guard is concerned with military defense of the United States, they have to be sure you are not a security risk to the country. Here you are fingerprinted. These remain part of your permanent record with the FBI.

Now it's time for lunch. You may eat for free in the MEPS dining room. If you wish to eat at a restaurant outside the building, you have to pay for your own meal.

The Coast Guard now knows more about you than when you first applied. Once more you talk to a career counselor, who will discuss your options based on your ASVAB results and your interests. The Coast Guard needs to be absolutely sure that

These recruits are waiting in line to receive the required tests for the Coast Guard physical exam.

you have made the right decision. One unhappy member of a small unit can be a disaster. These counseling sessions are for your benefit as well. Discuss freely what you want to do. You are not assigned to your specialty at this time unless you earned a guaranteed one.

Before leaving the MEPS, you take the oath of enlistment. This is a very solemn moment. You are pledging yourself to defend the country and to uphold its laws.

You are now part of the Coast Guard.

CHAPTER FIVE

BOOT CAMP

A few days, weeks or months after you've been sworn in, you leave with other new recruits for recruit training. All recruits go to the Coast Guard Station at Cape May, New Jersey.

It's scary, your first night in the **hall** (dormitory). You may be on your own and away from home for the first time in your life. You're surrounded by strangers in an unfamiliar place. Eager as you are to be in the Coast Guard, it's a culture shock. You ask yourself, "Was enlisting the right thing to do?"

Probably all the other recruits, men and women, are wondering the same thing. Before long, military life has become the norm for you. Those strangers are now your best friends. You take pride in one another's progress. Most importantly, you learn to work as a team. Once you are with a Coast Guard unit, you realize how vital that is.

Boot camp is tough—just as rugged for women as for men. You are one of 60 men and women who form a **company**. There are as many as 24 companies or as few as 16 training at the same time you are.

(Photo left)   For new recruits, boot camp often means rising before the sun.

You will arrive on a Tuesday. Before actual training begins on Thursday, your uniform will be issued to you. If you are a man, you have your hair cut. When the barber gets finished, you won't have much hair left! If you're a woman, your hair must be worn above the collar of your uniform.

Men and women sleep in the same hall, though in different sections or wings. One petty **officer** remembers there were only four women in her company. All women from all the companies in training at the same time sleep in the same section. Men bunk in the section assigned to their company.

During your eight weeks at Cape May, the most important person in your life is the company commander (C.C.). Your C.C., a regular who has served in the Coast Guard for more than one enlistment, has a gigantic responsibility. The C.C. is hard on you (and all the other recruits) because what you learn in boot camp may save your life.

You must be in top physical condition. The kinds of work you will do require physical strength, stamina and coordination. And so your C.C. makes you run, crawl, swim, climb and do push-ups until you're ready to drop.

Your training has to be intense. At any moment you may face action in any of the Coast Guard's missions. The Coast Guard emphasizes leadership. Are you able to take control in an emergency? The Coast Guard wants to know.

During boot camp you spend a lot of time in the classroom. You study such subjects as aids to navigation, law enforcement, uniforms and insignia, basic seamanship, first aid and much more. You discover the work involved in each of the Coast Guard missions. And you learn about the service's history.

The Coast Guard's history began back in 1790. The first secretary of the treasury, Alexander Hamilton, asked Congress to order the building of ten cutters (a type of ship). The first

Your company commander will provide training and advice that may one day save your life. Listen carefully and learn from your mistakes during your basic training period.

one, the *Massachusetts*, put to sea in 1791. These ships were used by the **Revenue Service** to prevent smuggling and collect fees for products being brought into the country.

In 1915 the **Cutter Service** (as it was then called) and the **Life Saving Service** became part of the Coast Guard. During

World War II the Coast Guard was transferred to the navy. It carried on antisubmarine, convoy escort, coastal defense and **amphibious** (land and sea) operations.

If there is one word to describe training at Cape May, it is "pressure." One **seaman** recruit, just graduated from boot camp, claims the work, the studies and the drills are difficult but it is the constant pressure that makes them extra hard. The attention to detail and the weekly tests worry every recruit.

"It all depends on your mental approach," he says. When the C.C. yells at you, *don't* blow up! *Never, but never, lose your temper.* Keep the right attitude. And if you graduate number one, you have first choice of available units. It's worth working for!

What will your **rating** (rank) be when you graduate? For the first three grades, **E-1** through **E-3**, you are a nonrate (you have no specialty). At first, you are a seaman recruit (E-1), your grade at basic. Then comes seaman apprentice (**E-2**). Usually you receive this promotion when you finish basic. A pay increase goes along with each promotion.

Before you reach the next higher grade, seaman (E-3), you must have served in your current rating for at least six months, have the approval of your commanding officer and show that you have the necessary qualifications.

While a nonrate, you are putting into use the many skills you learned at basic.

When you reach petty officer third class (**E-4**), you are no longer considered a nonrate. Now you can get on with a career in your specialty. To qualify for promotion from E-4 on up to **E-9**, master chief petty officer, you must also pass a Coast Guard test required for all those trying for that rating.

All enlisted personnel go through basic and serve with a unit, no matter what skill they specialize in later.

(Photo left) These recruits are working on the knot course at seamanship school.

CHAPTER SIX

YOUR FIRST DUTY STATION

Now you are ready for your first duty station. Before reporting, you have a ten-day leave (vacation).

Where will you be assigned? What will you do? How long will you be stationed there?

You may serve at a large base like those in Kodiak, Alaska, or Yorktown, Virginia. You may find yourself with a small unit, perhaps in a lonely place maintaining a **LORAN-C** installation. (You'll be there only a year.) LORAN-C stands for long-range navigation. You take part in one of the oldest Coast Guard missions.

A fleet of ships is needed to keep all the aids to navigation in good repair. These include lights marking channels, rivers, inland waterways, buoys and any dangerous areas—45,000 markers in all!

(Photo left)   These new members of the Coast Guard family have completed basic training and are looking forward to a ten-day rest before reporting to their prospective units.

This new recruit is shown remaking his bed after a company commander's inspection.

Your first job may be joining the crew on a 180-foot oceangoing or 65-foot river **tender** (a type of boat that supplies and "attends" the needs of other floating objects, such as navigational aids).

Your first duty station is not necessarily training for your career skill. Suppose you hope to become a public affairs specialist. Your first assignment might be to a unit doing iceberg patrol. Probably only when you reach petty officer third class (E-4) will you become a public affairs specialist.

While still with your first unit and a seaman apprentice (E-2), you can apply for specialized training in a Class "A" school.

But before you are ordered to that school, you must be promoted to a seaman rating (E-3). When you complete the Class "A" course in your specialty, your class ranking determines which of the available units you are free to choose as your next assignment. The units must have a vacancy in your new specialty.

Where will you live? There are three ways the Coast Guard provides housing. The first: You live on the base. This happens if you serve at large bases, during boot camp and at training centers (such as Class "A" schools).

The second way: The Coast Guard leases a local apartment. It is free housing for you and your family. The Coast Guard is your landlord. Sometimes, in fact, the whole apartment building is taken over by the Coast Guard.

You may live in a private home. The house is leased to the Coast Guard, just the way the apartment is. It is the same situation—free housing for you and your family. Your landlord is the government.

One petty officer says, "Although you live in and are part of the community, you're still leading a military life. That means your house undergoes thorough inspections, just as though you were living in a hall at boot camp."

There is a third way. You receive an allowance (money) from the Coast Guard and you find your own housing. Your living **quarters** (housing) are not inspected. You make your own arrangements with your landlord. It is almost like being a private citizen.

Although you will gain vast knowledge in the required training and educational programs, you will probably learn the most valuable skills through your own experience—at sea, on the job and in the service.

CHAPTER SEVEN

LIFE IN THE COAST GUARD

There is a big difference between going to work as a civilian and reporting for duty as a member of a Coast Guard unit.

You must, of course, wear a uniform. Your hours are 8:00 A.M. to 5:00 P.M. You may work in an office as a yeoman. Or as a seaman apprentice, you may assist a storekeeper and order clothing, foodstuffs and other items.

Don't forget, to perform the hard physical work of a seagoing unit, your team has to eat good, nourishing food. That's where the subsistence specialist comes in. As a seaman, you help with cooking, baking, preparing menus and keeping cost accounts, and you assist in ordering and inspecting foodstuffs.

If you are assigned to a small unit, your life is very different. Say you serve with a 30-person unit which usually does rescue

Coast Guard aircrews can search from the skies for drug smugglers or accident victims and then maneuver their helicopters into places boats can't go.

work. Your 44-foot motor lifeboat is made of metal, which crinkles and wrinkles instead of splitting apart.

Coast Guard personnel talk about being on a "two on, two off" schedule. Or if the unit is larger, it might be "one on, three off." Those are the number of 24-hour shifts you work. "Two on" means you are on duty for a total of 48 hours. Then you go home for 48 hours. Each unit varies.

At a small station half the personnel are usually on duty at all times. There is the officer of the day, who is in charge. He is probably a chief petty officer. The Coast Guard gives a lot of responsibility to **noncommissioned officers (noncoms)**.

If you are a woman you serve in all missions, even in search and rescue.

During your "on" days (duty days), after a normal workday you sleep in bunks at the station, watch TV, read, spend time in the recreation room, study, pursue a hobby or do whatever you wish.

Day and night you take your turn standing watch. You do the many chores necessary to keep your unit ready to act the second an emergency call is received.

Your boats must be clean and the engines working properly. Equipment must be checked. Has the medical kit been restocked since it was last used?

And then, just as you fall asleep in the bunk, the radio crackles: "Man overboard, lost at sea." You grab your boots and race to the dock. Will you save a life this time?

Coast Guard aviation is very active in search and rescue. Although pilots must be commissioned officers, there are five enlisted ratings open to you. If you're an aviation machinist's mate, you inspect aircraft equipment and prepare aircraft for flight. If you're an aviation electrician's mate, you maintain and repair lighting and electrical parts of aircraft controls.

Suppose you want to be a rescue swimmer. Then you must become an **aviation survivalman**. This is your career field. You jump from helicopters into freezing waters to save someone's life.

That's not all you do. You are responsible for being sure that parachutes are packed correctly. You are in charge of survival equipment. You must also pass **emergency medical training (EMT)**.

Are you extremely careful and accurate? If not, forget it. This type of aviation rescue work can only be done from choppers. No fixed-wing planes are used.

You can see that the Coast Guard is a very active service. A great many skills are required. You serve in a variety of ways. "What's it like," you wonder, "to be on iceberg patrol?"

The **International Ice Patrol** began in 1913 after a passenger ship (the *Titanic*) struck an iceberg and sank, resulting in many deaths. Other nations using the same sea routes (referred to as sea-lanes) help the Coast Guard patrol a 45,000-square-mile area. In an average year, the Coast Guard tracks between 200 and 500 icebergs and warns ships of the icebergs' positions. Some years, over 1,000 are seen!

But is it interesting to be on a ship sailing around icebergs? Yes, and it can be exciting too! There is always your ship to maintain. In addition, you frequently have interesting passengers. On board may be a scientist studying the formation, the travels and the breaking up of icebergs. Another scientist may be following weather patterns. And at any moment, day or night, you and your ship may be involved in a search and rescue operation.

CHAPTER EIGHT

SEMPER PARATUS

Here's an interesting and little-known fact about a very exciting part of Coast Guard duties. It is the duty of that service to inspect vessels believed to be carrying **contraband** (outlawed or illegal cargo).

These **boarding parties** are made up of various ratings and specialties. That means you can be a cook or a machinist's mate and still be part of a boarding party. You can be any rating. All members of the team have finished additional training in maritime (pertaining to the ocean) law enforcement.

After all, you have to know what laws you are enforcing, how to make an arrest and what to do with the illegal cargo. During the Persian Gulf conflict in the early months of 1991, many foreign ships were stopped and searched in the Persian Gulf. Even that far away from United States coastal waters, these searches were done by members of the Coast Guard.

Coast Guard members are shown here as they prepare to search a boat for illegal cargo.

You have another question: If you're assigned to a ship, do you spend your whole career at sea?

No. The Coast Guard has a **shore-float rotation**. If you are an **E-5** (petty officer second class) or a lower rating, you have a shore assignment for three years and a "float" assignment for three years. When you reach **E-6**, you have four years ashore for every three years afloat. Even when you are at sea, your vessel puts into port and you have time on shore.

You would like to try Coast Guard life but you're not sure you want to make it your career—not even for four years. How can that be done?

The Reserve is the answer. The requirements are the same as when you join the active Coast Guard. The same age limits—between 17 and 28—apply. So do the same citizenship regulations. Your enlistment is for eight years.

If you are a high school senior or attending a college or vocational school, you can join the **Student Reserve Program**. You are able to be in the reserve and not interrupt your schooling. You take your training during summer vacation.

All **reservists** go through basic training. If you don't have a skill that the Coast Guard needs, you attend a specialized training school (Class "A"). After that, you spend one weekend a month and two weeks a year working with an active service unit.

You take part in the duties of that unit. That means everything from port security to stopping commercial boats that have broken United States fishing laws to overseeing the cleanup of Mississippi River pollution.

In fact, the Coast Guard has four ratings (specialties) only for reservists: port securityman, data processing technician, investigator and fire safety technician.

In wartime you may be called into active service. In peacetime, if the Coast Guard needs someone with a skill you have, you will be asked to become active. You are not ordered. You are requested and are free to refuse.

What sort of skill could that be? One reservist who speaks Spanish was asked to serve on a ship for six months.

How can you tell a Coast Guard vessel from other ships? By its red slash! On April 6, 1967, a wide red bar, a narrow white stripe and a narrow blue one became the official markings of the Coast Guard. These are painted at an angle on the side of the ship toward the front. In the red is the Coast Guard emblem.

The Coast Guard has its own flag, called an **ensign**. An American eagle is in the upper left corner on a white rectangle. The rest of the ensign consists of red-and-white stripes with the emblem toward the lower right. So there's no excuse for not knowing a Coast Guard vessel when you see one!

Semper Paratus is the motto of the Coast Guard. As you can see, it lives up to the words "always ready."

Now you know more about the Coast Guard. There are jobs that sound exciting. There are other jobs, equally important, that can be dull. Your shore duty may be in an office—and you don't like filing! Maybe being called out any hour of the day or night in any kind of weather isn't as thrilling as you thought. There is no guarantee that you will take part in adventures.

Some of the stations are in lonely places. You may live far away from home and miss your family.

Should you join the Coast Guard? No one can decide for you. Think over the reasons why you should sign up. Then review the reasons why not. Only then will you be able to make an intelligent decision.

GLOSSARY

active reserve   A member of the active reserve is a civilian who serves part-time in the Coast Guard but has a regular full-time job.

active service   As a member of the active service, the Coast Guard is your only job. You are a full-time member of the Coast Guard.

amphibious   Pertaining to both land and water.

Armed Services Vocational Aptitude Battery (ASVAB)   A test required of everyone who hopes to join one of the armed services.

aviation survivalman   You take special training in how to save people in emergency situations. Your training includes rescue swimming and giving emergency medical aid.

base   Government-owned property or property being used by one of the armed services.

basic training   The first instruction you receive after reporting for duty.

boarding party   Members of a team who leave their ship, go onto another vessel believed to be carrying outlawed or illegal cargo and search that vessel.

boot camp   Same as basic training.

civilian   Someone not in one of the armed services.

Class "A" school   Technical school for advanced training after basic training.

commissary   Supermarket.

company   A unit of 60 men and women.

contraband   Outlawed or illegal products.

Cutter Service   Early name for Coast Guard.

Delayed Entry Program   A program for putting off (delaying) your reporting for active service after you have enlisted.

emergency medical training (EMT)   Part of training for an aviation survivalman.

ensign   A flag.

Entrance National Agency Checks (ENTNAC)   The agency that checks your background to be sure you are not a security risk to the United States.

E-1, E-2, E-3, up to E-9   Pay grades. They are the same for all the armed services.

hall   Building where you sleep and keep your possessions during basic training.

inactive reserve   The period remaining on your enlistment contract after you have finished your active service is spent in the inactive reserve. You can be called to duty during a war but you have no other Coast Guard duties during peacetime.

International Ice Patrol   Personnel assigned to this duty track icebergs and warn ships of the icebergs' positions.

Life Saving Service   Became part of the Coast Guard in 1915.

LORAN-C   Long-range aids to navigation.

maritime   Having to do with the sea.

Military Entrance Processing Station (MEPS)   The place where you take your physical, pass a security check, decide the type of work you hope to do in the Coast Guard, sign the enlistment contract and take the oath.

Montgomery G.I. Bill   A Congressional bill that provides a way for you to continue your education.

noncommissioned officer (noncom)   An enlisted person from the rating (rank) of petty officer third class on up.